EINSTEIN'S BRAIN

UNIVERSITY OF UTAH PRESS POETRY SERIES

RICHARD CECIL

EINSTEIN'S BRAIN

UNIVERSITY OF UTAH PRESS   SALT LAKE CITY   1986

University of Utah Press Poetry Series
Dave Smith, *Editor*

See Acknowledgments, page 79, for permission statements.

∞ The paper in this book meets the standards for permanence
and durability established by the Committee on Production Guidelines
for Book Longevity of the Council on Library Resources.

Library of Congress Cataloging-in-Publication Data

Cecil, Richard, 1944–
    Einstein's brain.

    (University of Utah Press poetry series)
    I. Title.   II. Series.
PS3553.E32E36   1986   811'.54   86-1607
ISBN 0-87480-255-5 (alk. paper)

for Maura

CONTENTS

III

I

VENICE

One morning, driving Tucson's widest street
miraged by waves of heat into a river,
maneuvering my dark imported car
through heavy traffic past cinder-block motels,
I remembered the Grand Canal in Venice,
marble-flanked and opening on sea,
when suddenly I realized that Venice,
California, facing the Pacific,
cool and foggy,
was just five hundred miles ahead through desert.

Since I was running way behind again
to my temporary job as gadget salesman
at Tucson's Newest Discount Showroom Store,
the shadowy line of mountains dead ahead
called to me more loudly than my duty,
though engine clatter drowned out every sound
in traffic but the local desert music,
the roaring stereos of open cars;
for mountains call
the inner ear with music of the spheres.

And, though ugliness has greater force,
beauty's more persistent; for example,
the trailer court beyond the low motels,
wedged between the suburbs and the mountains,
looked already ancient — bleached bone white
and occupied by ghosts whose aging cars,
dry-rotted inside and faded by the glare,
were stalled by double-wide, immobilized
mobile homes
sure to be outlasted by the mountains.

So when I reached the Foothills Shopping Center
in crawling traffic, half an hour late,
instead of taking the turnoff into FED-MART
like almost every car in front of me,
I stayed on the road, which narrowed, curved,
and rose above the condominiums,
Italian Restaurant, and gangsters' mansions
to a sixty-mile vista at its crest
uninterrupted
perhaps to Venice, by human ugliness.

For, instead of rows of concrete houses,
this valley subdivided into rows
of desert vegetation spaced as neatly
as Paris' *Jardin d'Acclimatation* —
lines of spiny cholla and prickly pear
alternating with the mesquite trees,
whose low and twisted branches and tiny leaves
were like the window bars on Tucson's houses,
adaptations
ugly but necessary in this desert.

Up there on Vista Point I hesitated,
estimating if my half a tank
of gasoline, my overheated engine,
my treadless tires, my battery on discharge
were sufficient to carry me through that landscape
without a single human blot upon it
from my summit to the next jagged range
except the road itself, the road to Venice,
narrow and hostile
as the slender causeway to Italian Venice.

Former warlike dukedom, walled by sea,
approachable by gondola or rail,
the city looks today exactly like
the city of Giorgione and of Titian,
but hurry! it's sinking in the Adriatic!
my guidebook said; but though I still remember
electric yoyo salesmen in the square
and private speedboats hogging the canals,
marble Venice,
doomed, seemed not as doomed as this landscape.

Behind me, oatmeal stucco buildings climbed
halfway up the ridge, and way, way ahead,
beyond Los Angeles, the ocean lapped
the rotting pilings of the Venice dock
while gulls patrolled the crowded shoreline
screaming for a handout but getting none —
gray fog, gray faces, gray peeling houses,
and gray, bone-chilling surf concealing sharks,
gray and white,
predatory as Venice cocaine dealers.

Looking east, behind me, way below,
at FED-MART's lot, filling up despite me,
I wondered if a person had been found
to stand behind my counter for my pay
while I stood up here wasting time, wavering
between my pretty past and fading present
and ugly ugly ugly ugly future,
trying to choose between two Venices,
one sinking,
one hideous; Reader, I went nowhere.

THE MIDDLE CLASS

Upstairs we pace from room to room,
dazzled by the view of trees
even from the bathroom's window.
I point out pretty, turning leaves

whose names I say I can't remember,
although I learned them years ago
on my field trip to the woods
in Municipal Zoo and Arboretum.

Bussed with other city children
through a neighborhood so dangerous
the driver made us lock our windows
in that September's record heat,

I started at the unfamiliar street
of tenements and bars and pawnshops.
Children lounging on the curb
gazed back at me with vacant eyes.

I'd never seen that kind of look.
I thought it meant indifference
until I cracked my window open
secretly at a traffic light.

They thrust their fists into the gap,
jabbing my cheeks and teeth and chin
and neck. Jesus, they were fast.
I slammed my window down on nothing.

Later, as I trooped through aisles
of Sumac, Walnut, Tulip Poplar,
I tried to memorize their leaves
by taping them into my sketchbook.

I filed that book till Christmas Eve,
saving the reds and golds and yellows
as a present to myself. But when I opened,
the leaves were uniformly gray.

I tried to match the names to shapes,
but outline's all I'd saved of leaves.
Staring at the disappointing page,
I remembered those blank faces:

I see them still, peering in
the windows of my dream streetcars
to downtown Baltimore at night.
I'm six. The windows will not shut.

Now, gazing from our second story
at these lovely, nameless shapes, I'm sorry
all I learned to recognize
was hate. My trees are naked sticks.

ELEGY FOR BALTIMORE

I stagger from the Oriole Tavern
toward my little foreign car
with its out-of-state license plates
parked beneath the doughboy's statue
in the corner near the freshest grave
inside the Veterans Cemetery.
I look up into his bronze face,
cruelly mottled by the pigeons,
and think of my two years' service
as a typist in the States.
Comrade, what we have endured!

We've traveled to and passed the limits
of our enormous continent
on public and on private business —
driven, flown, been shipped across
ice-choked northern seas to fight
customs, Germans, in peace and war,
and won. We sweated out enlistments,
yours in trenches, mine in barracks,
yours in Paris, mine in Athens,
Georgia, defeating fear and boredom.
Demobilized, we hurried home.

I flew first class with bonus money
back to our native Baltimore,
not nostalgic — I hated home
almost since my birth and begged,
as soon as I had learned to talk,
my stepfather, every Sunday, to please
please drive me to the state line —
but I needed to return to zero
to rewind the raveled skein
I'd never wind again. I thought
my next departure would be my last.

But you sailed back in a cypress box
deep within the ship that hauled
above you on its decks the troops
whose terrible load of living hope
pressed the steel hull deep
into the cold Atlantic. You rode
light. You floated on death's surface
as supple as an experienced mariner,
while fellow passengers tossed and retched
from Le Havre to Baltimore harbor.
But they're all dead now, too, here

in ports of earth with granite anchors
to hold them steady in the storms
of renovation blowing down
the ugly buildings we remember
to be replaced with uglier ones
which they and I will never see,
but which your x-ray stare will bore
as now it bores through me, departing.
When the rest of Baltimore is gone,
like me, over your horizon,
what a lovely view you'll have of nothing.

THE WANDERER

> "I am a stranger everywhere."
>> Frank Schubert, "The Wanderer"

Is this going to be my home? I ask myself
in morning light too dull to contrast faces
of motorists in gray coats with collars
darkened by freezing rain. They walk hunched
around their centers of gravity for balance,
holding their umbrellas like tightrope walkers.
They shuffle from the gas pumps to the rest rooms
head down, ignoring the listlessness of the sun.

Can I be one of them? I'm in my car,
in brilliant domelight, tracing Interstates
north and east along my U.S. map.
Under my wool shirt my skin is burned
from Arizona, where I watched burglars case
my neighborhood in jogging shorts this Christmas.
Returning New Year's to my ransacked house,
I inventoried worthless things and packed

and drove against the motion of the sun
till mountains flattened into eastern plains,
which years before I'd smiled to see grow dim
and disappear in my rearview mirror.
Back then, I stamped down on the accelerator
to gain momentum for the steep incline.
Now, I'm pulled off in a service station
waiting for sleet to change to rain or stop.

The local cars keep going. It's Monday morning;
work's their destination. I have no job.
I'm expected nowhere. I read my map
and wait. Later, I'll drive on ice like them.
Or will I turn back south or west again,
looking for a landscape and a climate
less brutal than the city I was born in,
or any atmosphere I've breathed since then?

For though, just now, I left my car to trudge
through unfamiliar slush, familiar chill
now penetrates my skin. I search my map
for X's blotting places I have been:
Here, people leave you alone; there, sun;
here, ice; there, dust falling constantly.
This wanderer's a stranger everywhere,
though everywhere's a ghastly kind of home.

EXILE

The unfamiliar stair to rented rooms
creaks musically, and though the panes are greasy,
the view is new. Outside, strange birds sing;
inside, heat pipes rattle out a tune.
Reaching for a light switch in the dark,
hands brush velvet drapes instead of plaster.
Tossing on a worn out, borrowed mattress,
lovers fall into the grooves of lovers
and sleepers fall into the grooves of sleepers
so that, for days or weeks or sometimes months,
dreams and sex are memorable. But then
the arms and legs cut channels of their own,
hands lose feeling, ears deafen, and then,
without returning, exiles end at home.

GENRE PAINTING

My maple didn't turn
this fall to red or gold;
its withered leaves just paled
to jaundiced green and fell.
Now I'm raking wildly
to meet the vacuum sweeper
crawling up my street,
where piles of neighbors' leaves
from rainbow colored oaks,
catalpas, tulip poplars
lie neatly stacked at curbside.
For neighbors understood
the meaning of the headline
in *City News* last night:
TOMORROW'S AUTUMN ROUNDUP.
It made no sense to me
as I glanced at mastheads
of all the daily papers
in automatic vendors
outside the liquor store.
If I had had the change
I would have bought the *Times*,
not the local paper,
to read about our newest
undeclared small war —
how many died, and why.
But since I had no quarters
I found out less than neighbors
who only read the *News*
delivered to their houses —
zoning fights, divorces,
battles on the Council.
They may have been discussing
these latest local wars
at six o'clock this morning,

but I couldn't hear their talk
above the nerve destroying
scrape of rakes on concrete
waking me at dawn,
which I took to be the screech
of air raid sirens, real ones
ending my dream of war
with war. The time and season
seemed perfect for the death
of pale, autumnal peace.
I walked to my window,
naked but strangely hot,
and peered around the blind.
I saw a red horizon —
just as I'd imagined,
but only red with dawn,
only fired by sun.
I saw my leafless maple
backed by the solar disk.
Stripped, it looked as good
as neighbors' cared-for trees.
I'll water it next summer;
I'll weed my ragged lawn
I thought. My heart was lifted
by the sight of neighbors
who stretched from end to end
of First Street — my street — raking
like peasants in a painting:
AUTUMN ROUNDUP DAY,
sixteenth century Dutch,
school of Pieter Brueghel.
See their fat red faces?
I'll be one next year
frisking up the leaves
from our lovely scarlet trees,
whose blackened skeletons
looming over us
will be the only hint
of the approaching plague.

THE INTERRUPTED NAP

Central air recirculates the room
raising little hairs along my arms
exactly as they rise when, almost asleep,
alone, I stroke them with my fingertips.
I'm so accustomed to touching you at night
that in this dark I've made at noon with drapes
drawn against the terrible August sun,
I automatically reach for something smooth,
skinlike: the velvet chairback, the cat, my wrist.

I run my nails along the lines of veins
as lightly as the manufactured wind
runs along the surfaces of this room,
cooling them. I close my eyes. I shiver.
I sink down into the sofa's cushions
like a diver in a deep-sea bell:
outside, savage atmospheres; inside,
the delicate networks of blood and nerves; between,
thin walls of steel, of glass, of skin.

I remember almost drowning. In early evening,
blinding sunset reflected in the pool,
I dove incautiously into the shallow end
and dashed my head against the concrete rim.
I could have breached the surface with my hand,
but so cool and dark and absolutely quiet
the bottom seemed, I knew that I was miles
below my playmates' faces peering down.
When the lifeguard fished me with her hook,

I rose by the stretched elastic of my trunks
into the noise and heat and light, amazed,
for I thought that I had slipped all nets.
When she firmly pressed her lips to mine
to force her breath into my emptied chest,
I fought. I clamped my teeth so desperately
she had to prize them open with a stick.
Oxygen burned like acid in my lungs.
Next day, I bragged about my first French kiss.

At six, I didn't want to owe my life.
But thirty years later, waiting for you
in the artificial dark, I forgive her
harsh resuscitation. She couldn't know
how pleasantly my shroud of water wrapped me,
how snug my coffin of endless sleep, how often,
abandoned for an afternoon, nothing
half as pleasant as almost drowning happens,
until you shove the door against its jam,

pouring heat and light and noise inside.
And I don't criticise your rough embrace.
We lucky divers always wake to violence,
tons of gravity hurled down on us, furious
congratulations shouted in our ears.
Silence is the consolation of the lost.
Self-sufficiency. They've cut the line by which
anyone could haul them in. I envy them.
Then I envy no one, waking in your arms.

DEATH

Today my mail's so dull I open
my wife's Annuity Newsletter —
it's *ours*, not *hers*, I tell myself —
and read its featured story: You,
Retirement, Money, Work, and Death.

On page one's chart of mortality
I x the crossing of my Life line
with my Cash Accumulation curve:
I'm going to die a millionaire
two years after I retire . . .

But no, I've read the columns wrong.
I'm not *Annuitee*,
I'm *Dependent*, so I will die
way down here, a decade later
than *Spouse* who works himself to death;

but I will have to live on nothing
after death destroys the *Breadwinner*
and inflation kills my million dollars.
My working neighbors will die or move
southwest to die in warmer places,

while I'll survive to see their houses
decay into unpainted rentals.
And if I live as long as scheduled,
I'll live to be my only tenant,
senile slumlord to myself.

But my awful future's brighter
than the futures of hard workers
according to the interviews
with retired survivors — widows
and widowers — which follow the statistics.

For the loneliest, most bored respondents
agree that work's a kind of death —
an active death where the body's chained
to a desk or some incessant machine
while the heart is rended by desire

to do nothing. To sleep dreamless.
Everybody but the dead —
who were not interviewed, of course —
prefers the poverty of leisure
to renumerated work.

Only death is worse than work,
says one embittered retiree,
complaining of a heart condition
contracted on his awful job.
He's sixty-seven, due to die . . .

No more of this morbid little tabloid!
I say, and carry it to the fireplace.
But tossing it in the kindling box
on top of a pile of daily papers
I notice they too headline death —

from EIGHTY KILLED IN ANDES CRASH
in page one's boldest type
to *Poet Dies on Taxi Ride*
in *Arts & Travel*'s small italics.
Such deaths are just bad luck,

I think, not like a pencil-line's
remorseless, predictable advance
across the graph of my existence.
If I book passage on the wrong plane
or hail a cab that death climbs in,

my improvidential life
(I've never made a "living wage"
or held a steady job for long)
will end without diminishment
of income, without the space between

the job of life and the job of death.
For isn't death a kind of work —
a bad, but regular employment
with twenty-four hour, seven-day shifts
and no vacations? Such work is hell,

but *retirement's simply heaven*, I read,
glancing down one last time
at the page I've just decided to burn
right now, to start a fire
to chase September's early cold —

though leaves are still a violent green
on the dogwood and the maple tree
the former owner of my house
planted in his front yard —
mine, now — to watch grow taller

while he rose through his life's stages,
advancing to the intersections
of money, work, retirement, death.
His trees survive, but they'll burn soon
to stint death's never-ending chill.

SEPTEMBER SONNET

I'm lying here unhappy in the gloom
because the other half of Earth is bright
while my half has to shiver in the dark;
for winter, summer, day and night are split
between two hemispheres. It's your spring now,
São Paulo, and your dawn, Pago Pago.
But as you walk out on your balconies
in thin nightgowns, Brisbane, Sidney, Melbourne,
think of North America's newest winter.
Our summer failed again, but so will yours,
because the world's unfairer than it seems:
So much heat for you, so much for me,
like a bone between two dogs, until it's snatched
by death, and we lie always dark and cold.

NIGHT SCHOOL

My second year on First Street,
my twentieth year from home,
the house that I was born in
is still my house in dreams,
so that, just now, waking,
I have to feel my way
along the bedroom wall
to find my door and light switch.
And no one from this town
or any town I've lived
in exile from my childhood
ever calls in dreams;
I meet with only dead
or decades absent friends.
The dead ones lecture me
on the difference between
my life, their death: *Not much,*
they tell me; *food and sex,*
now and then a movie,
barely compensate
for your daily loss of hope,
your ever harder heart.
The living come more rarely;
most have forgotten me.
But tonight my classmates
from elementary school,
all grown to monster size,
squeezed behind their desks,
told me their life stories.
The prettiest girl, a nun,
said she's loved me always,
was dreaming of me now
inside her cloister cell.

But when she leaned toward me
in her enveloping black veil,
a lock of graying hair
fell forward on her brow.
I turned to my best friend
to ask him where he'd been
since our argument
thirty years ago.
But his face was twisted
with implacable rage,
for he had hated me
faithfully for years.
I turned toward the window
sheeted with gray rain
so dense the classroom seemed
to be an aquarium.
A stream of water ran
in a channel in the floor,
with transparent fish
gliding in its current.
I plunged my hand at them
but they slipped my grasp.
My classmates, one by one
stepped into that stream.
The mermaid girls blew kisses.
My friend became an eel
and all swam off and left
me still in school at forty.
Then a splash of rain
from gutters choked with leaves
woke me from this dream.
How I long to float
back into that classroom!
but can't — my heart's a stone.

WIDOWER

November, the house across the street emerged
behind its row of leafless maples. Tonight,
an old man framed in its second story window
peers in my direction, but I'm hidden
behind a fence of bushy evergreens
which screen my room in winter as in summer.

I'm sad, I'm lonely, he's saying to himself
staring from his yellow lighted window.
I cannot hear his voice but his lips
move and though I cannot read his lips,
there's nothing else to say alone at evening
leaning toward a locked pane, undressing,

except please snow please snow please snow please snow,
which is my own address to the inky sky.
Please stitch closed the rifts in pine branches
before the dolefullness across the street
blossoms into detail — wrinkled stockings
and empty perfume bottles on the dresser;

the dead wife's picture by the mirror;
her forgotten slippers under the bed,
tangled with dustballs; her out-of-fashion dresses
hung in plastic cases in the closet
between his bathrobe and his mackintosh —
tulle and organdy and silk, green and pink . . .

Technically, I'm blind without my glasses
but I don't need binoculars to see
across the hundred yards between us.
In a drawer of nightgowns he never opens
there's a leather album of photographs
whose bronze clasp is locked. The key's lost,

for pictures of his parents don't need review:
In high collars their young, stern faces
stare from dreams; their terrible eyes glitter
at him from mirrors when he combs his hair.
In pictures he's the toddler in suspenders.
In life he's a wrinkling face within a glass

a neighbor, a stranger has to look away from
even at this distance, safely hidden
behind this one-way mirror of the pines.
For though the snow has mercifully begun to fall
in every window, making my young wife sing
downstairs, that's me, or her, in thirty years.

GUILT

Take back my chicken-mushroom stew
and put some chicken in it please,
I practice saying to myself,
but when the waitress brings the check
and asks us how we like the food,
I see her glance so nervously
at our uneaten meals, I choke
my anger down and answer, *Fine.*
For all around us empty booths
testify that dinners here
are always just as bad as ours;
I know that any likely action
taken in this place's kitchen
won't fix deliberate mistakes
like no cheese in cheese and spinach pie.
The coffee's instant, the wine's vinegary,
the candlesticks are candleless.

I want us just to pay and leave,
but when you show your dirty fork,
I decide to be assertive.
So we send our dinners back
and wait another half an hour
to taste inedible revisions
of hopeless, botched originals
before we mercifully agree
we ought to skip our free desserts.
We leave a thirty percent tip —
not satirically enormous,
but large enough to blunt the curse
of being waitress here, I hope.
We're her only customers;
she locks the exit door behind us.

We cross the street to THE DAILY GRIND
for fresh coffee, fresh cheesecake —
or stale if stale is all you've got,
you tell the grinning waiter. We eat;
we order more; we lick our plates.
This cheesecake becomes the happy end
of the Story of the Awful Restaurant
we'll tell each other for years and years
until one dies and the other forgets —
a funny story that doesn't end,
except in my mangled private version,
with the sobbing cook and waitress
scraping our plates into the garbage,
starving in their restaurant
while I wipe sugar from my lips.

CAREERS

One day at work I shuffled through brochures,
searching for the desert or the tundra
too desolate to support a small ambition,
or any industry but imagination,
where the richest house was made of ice or canvas
and its destruction by the wind or sun
delighted the Eskimo or Bedouin
too long confined within its tiny circuit.
But only earthquake or atomic war
could've swept away our bungalow

built low and small of fireproof double brick.
There, you were staring through the picture window
at airplanes disappearing in the smog.
You had been leafing through brochures of jungles
looking for a pink, impossible hotel
with toucans lodged in its cultivated palms,
water lilies in its swimming pool.
Now, lavish chambers unfolded in your brain
as sunset dimmed our all-white living room,
whose walls we left so absolutely bare

you were the only color, the only figure
I saw when I pushed in the door that evening.
You looked like a woman by Vermeer,
gold in golden light, all dark around,
and I too, lit up. Now I can't remember,
easing the U-Haul down our narrow drive,
those moderate few years of dim success,
but just that momentary flash of insight
such as must have passed from Isabella
to Columbus: love of brilliant failure.

ABSTINENCE

Years ago I sipped three drinks
every evening in the thickening shade
and felt the sunshine spread across my skin

about the time of the rising of the moon
through dense clouds over dark hills,
lighting them as much as sun at dawn.

I happened to reverse life's normal cycle.
Instead of sleep and work and recreation
determined by the angle of the sun

I rose to the level of the gin each night
and set with the setting of my martini glass
into the lukewarm water in the dishpan.

But once I happened to find myself awake
and staring at morning's glum illumination
through a tear in always drawn curtains.

I assumed at first that I was dreaming,
for I could not identify the shapes
of offices except by window lights,

nor could I recognize the unlit streets
lined with houses I had never seen,
swarming with strangers I had only heard

humming in the twilight, heading home,
their work done just as mine began.
Now they all were silent, grim, and marching

out of step to the beat of heavy traffic
clogging every thoroughfare and alley —
an overwhelming tide that lapped around

and left no avenue of silence for me,
all wrapped and muffed against the outer cold,
to slide away on, even in my brain

to the deep, cold lake I imagined
in the center of my city's night landscape,
obliterated by the day's mirage:

No blue-white snow-drift blurry shore,
no cries of skaters testing thin ice
with their weightless bodies, razor edges.

— So this is really real life — I thought.
That night the lake returned, but dark shapes
swam under every inch of frozen surface,

for now my glass was filled with only water,
my curtain had been spread, my window opened:
I recognized the night as night and chose it.

II

AT THE FRANKLIN PLANETARIUM

"The stars, like us, are temporary lights,"
said the tape-recorded voice. "They're born,
they mark their brilliant passages, they die,
although we steer by Columbus's constellations,
as Columbus steered by Leif Erickson's."

We bent our seatbacks nearly horizontal
to see the Philadelphia sky unroll
its winter aspect on the blackening dome.
Although I had rarely more than glanced at stars
I saw at once the falseness of this projection:

They were too bright by many magnitudes;
the dark between them lacked its hint of blue.
I thought, they'd look like this from Mars to us
as we peered through some city's plastic roof
and listened to the meteors ping against it —

the way we had stared up in the dark and listened,
that long first night together in our house,
when wind drove sleet against our skylight,
testing the seamless thickness of the glass.
And though we pressed as close as skin to bone

a furious isolation slipped between us —
not like the sword shy lovers press between them,
but like the thin cold blade of atmosphere
separating stars. We each, alone,
imagined how the shattered pane would fall,

mixed with ice, jagged on our faces.
We lay like that till just before the dawn,
when the clouds, shredded by the wind,
opened just above our ceiling. A crowd of stars
shone through the gap. They would have looked

like those around the dome — blue white, gigantic,
steady aids to explorers' navigation
until they fail, like us, spectacularly alone —
except the skylight, piled with melting sleet,
bent each point of light into a rainbow.

It turned our bodies into bright reflections
of every color except the white of stars
and the black of the empty spaces in between.
How gorgeously we sparkled on the sheets
before the dawn, and sleep, erased us.

THE RELIEF MAP

When I hold the desk lamp
sideways to Alaska
this avenue of palms
is shadowed by that glacier.
The Gulf of Mexico
and the Bering Sea
are thumbsized blue depressions
marking the north/south margins.
Mercatorial distortion
flattens Kansas, stretches
Texas to a handspan —

everyplace looks the same
as in my flying dreams.
Arizona's brown;
California slides
into its ocean. And cities
glitter taxi-yellow
whatever their elevation.
I loom above them,
a million times enlarged,
tracing hair-thin lines
drawn between their names.

Why so many Salems?
Portlands? In the gray
south-central plain
Athens rises four times,
a hundredth of an inch
above its flat horizons.
But where the lines grow crooked
on the spiky ridges
and disappear, there,
the faint black names
buried in mountain green

sing. They lay themselves
along the dead-end lines
in anapestic strings:
Taylor, Shumway, Snowflake,
Show Low, Cloud, Morenci,
Indian Pine, Pinetop, Pine,
Big Stone Gap.
I'd shrink a million times
to scaled-down human size
to see a Hannigan Meadows
as wonderful as its name.

But when, at dawn this morning,
I drove into these mountains
looking for a Swiss chalet,
I found a sad hotel
overlooking a strip mine.
— So that's the Copper Queen —
I said, and drove relentlessly
back the way I'd come,
past the Alpine Lodge,
the Grey Shadows Inn,
McNary, Greer, Mt. Airy —

God, what ugliness! —
until I reached, again,
this continental shelf
that slopes, without a wrinkle
into the Arctic Circle.
Where to? — I asked myself.
Cairo, Illinois?
Manhattan, Kansas?
Mesopotamia, Ohio?
Their dots line one route
I might, in desperation,

take before I take
the route so clearly marked
when I flip the map
to its white, concave reverse.
That's the mirror country,
monochrome and featureless,
without a town or highway,
which rises to my feet,
my tires, and the windows
that used to be my eyes,
covering like a blanket.

FREDERICKSBURG

The drone of mowers in the cemetery
reminds me that the grass grows constantly
while I doze in this high, oak-paneled room.
Up and down the street the neighbors' dogs
bark the way that birds, elsewhere, sing,
but not from fear or hunger or to issue warnings —
just to punctuate the silences
between cicada shrieks. Yet it's quiet
enough to sleep with doors and windows open.

But I mustn't, yet. I have to cut my lawn,
greened by rain and by the unofficial,
unmarked who lie outside the graveyard.
Since they didn't figure in the battle
either as entrenched and walled defenders
or as the suicidal stormers of the hill,
they weren't buried with enemies or friends,
but abandoned to the swamp in which they drowned
while ducking terrible artillery.

Most were floated by the tide downriver
or drifted over to the northern shore.
But the mangled or dismembered ones
sank in shell holes below the seepage level,
where they could not be shot or drowned again,
nor found, later, when the swamp was drained
to make this line of houses and that graveyard,
its headstones dressed in military rows
and carved with names, dates, and regiments.

Under those stones lie the soldiers
who died obeying their commanders' orders.
Over here, below foundations of the houses,
lie the dead who died obeying orders
issued from within: *Run! Hide!*
These were heroes of the small republics
bounded and defended by their skins;
thus no monument's raised to them.
They probably prefer to be forgotten.

But I have got to mow the lawn above them,
soon — it's late, the dogs bark now at crickets,
and the basement sump pump just switched on,
as it does each evening. It pumps rain
that fell a century ago on them.
By settling down on their uncoffined bones,
this house I live in is their mausoleum,
until the swamp retakes this bottomland,
erasing minor life and death distinctions.

WHAT CHEER, IOWA

Arriving in a town with no hotel,
I gazed through the window of the train
at houses I'd have to buy or rent
if I stepped down to the platform.
Rain cascaded from the sloped roofs.
I tossed a paper cup and watched it
catch up in the gutter's current
and sail doughtily past the gas station
and the Sparkle Cleaners, past
the dozen white frame bungalows.
A boy, the town's only visible resident,
fired bb's at it from his porch
but missed, for it did not veer.
It rode lightly, like an empty ship,
to where the street narrowed to a highway.
There, in a shoal of broken concrete,
it snagged beneath the RESUME SPEED sign,
held steady, filled with rain, and sank.
The stream ended just beyond,
washing down an open manhole.
But the road, without rise or bend
except the earth's slight curve down,
continued to the limits of my vision.
Cows dotted that horizon.
Huddled backwards to the wind,
they laid their heavy bodies down
in the muddy field and vanished.
Clouds sank behind the cows.
Twenty-five thousand miles beyond
where the clouds touched down
the town would rise again, I thought.
Its one street. Its boy
firing the volley of welcome. And I
would lean against this window,
sick to death of travel, and stare
at these same twelve houses in the rain,
relieved that none would take me in.

EDISON IN FLORIDA

I stand here dressed in shorts, half asleep
from listening to the tour guide's droning voice
before she plays the famous first recording,
and wonder if that energetic man
regretted being rich enough to leave
New Jersey, full of ignorance and night,
the raw materials for his inventions,
to relocate down here among distractions —
a young new wife, dear Henry Ford next door.
They must have made his sixteen-hour days
inside this windowless arc-lighted lab,
surrounded by a jungle garden, seem longer
than December days he spent in Menlo Park
inventing light. *What's Florida without?*
he must have asked himself each scented dawn
as he trudged by blooming orange trees,
gardenias, begonias, in his worsted suit.

I like to think that on his final visit,
he took his coat off when he reached this office,
draped it on this swivel chair, leaned back
and thought about the past and not the future
for the first time. I do not think he closed
his eyes — I don't when I'm trying to remember.
No, he stared into the ceiling fixture
to blind himself with light, to see white only
as, in boyhood summer, he tried to stare
straight up into the brilliant August sun.
Then, what rare, unplayable regret
did he record on cylinder of heart?
I'm staring now into that same lamp —
the bulb's original, has burned for decades.
I wonder, did he think it consolation
to be survived by his inventions, as song
survives the dead recording artist? I don't.

STEERSMAN'S VOYAGE

Ulysses' ship receded
faster than I could swim
toward its whirling oars,
so I veered off its course
through cold green waves
toward familiar shore,
and followed the warm blue current,
crowded with dolphins, out.
My language was so common
the fish nearest the surface
probably understood me
when I asked directions
to their continent,
but never opened mouths
except to eat each other.
And though the resting sea gulls
bobbing on the waves
chattered constantly,
they were as occupied
with fishing as the fish.
Therefore I had to travel
without expert advice
to the suburbs of Atlantis
where, being unknown
and silent as an eel,
I was thought a native
in costume of that country —
iridescent skin,
naked, seaweed hair.
The herons on its towers
dived and dived at me
slowly through the water
as I passed their gates.
At every intersection
slouched a grinning shark;

the esplanade was crowded
with cruising barracuda;
every other building
lining the wavy streets
seemed a banquet house
whose feasters stared at me
with their lidless eyes
through the pane-less windows.
The shipwrecked prostitutes
lounging around the harbor
reached for me with fingers
all bone, tendonless.
The kiss one begged of me
was all teeth. I didn't
like her ivory touch
at first, but oh how difficult
to keep oneself intact
so deep so far from home
where no familiar custom
but appetite survives.
And so I laced with her
in anemone designs
woven by the tide —
spiraled legs and arms,
labyrinthine traps
for fish who licked me clean.
Oh voyager, don't fear!
They flickered like my heart
inside my cage of ribs;
they beat and beat like waves
against my bony chest
with perpetual desire,
just as the sirens sing.

SHIPWRECKS

Nags Head, Oct., 1981

Where land ends and sea begins I find
a line of condominiums and decide
I want this kind of money — summer house,
martinis on the redwood deck at twilight
after jogging with the golden retriever
up and down the sunset painted beach,
many hundred miles from city neon,
which fades the sky to illuminate the streets.
Here, lamps are properly set in darkness.
Shoreward, cars light narrow strips of blacktop;
seaward, marina buoys blink red and green,
marking out the path for yachts, and overhead,
airport searchlights substitute for stars
to guide the private planes through harbor fog.
By the inward glow of blue aquariums,
lobsters swim in seafood restaurants.

But I was guided by picture window light
from houses and apartments strung for miles.
I stand on someone's private dune and spin
one hundred and eighty degrees from shore to ocean,
blurring the artificial lights to streaks;
but they've already killed my night vision.
My back to houses, I see black on black,
dizzy with the absence of a point —
comet, constellation — on which to fix,
while way, way out a lost sailor
mistakes this dazzling coast behind me
for his deep water port and crams his wheel
hard over, toward the shallow inlet,
while I blindly follow the sound of surf
beyond NO TRESPASSING, KEEP OUT, and DANGER signs.
We both founder on the public rocks.

THE AIRPORT OF THE COUNTRY OF THE BLIND

Every month is February. No sun or stars
penetrate the clouds, whose rain by day
and sleet by night substitute for clocks.
In droughts we burn our streetlights
constantly, unsure that twelve strokes
mean noon or midnight. After a week
of dryness the graveyard shift
collides with children taking recess,
so we don't complain when moisture
chokes our lungs, or wail for spring.
Were spring to come, the sun
fall once through a rift of sky,
the skim of ice that substitutes for eyes
would break, light leak into our brains.

Yet I wish I could tear through to it.
I doze in the lobby of our airport
as the announcer cancels flight after flight,
half listening for the defiant pilot
to start his plane. The fog's too thick
to read the numbers on its tail and wings.
I touch its glowing instruments —
radar to bounce off our hidden mountains,
altimeter to measure our soaring grayness —
aren't they eyes enough? The pilot sighs
for his dog and white cane. But someday
I will make him fly me, or dream he flew me
beyond the barrier of this air and ground
to brilliance, which we'll know by touch —
its lightness, its heat, our shattered faces.

THE UMBRELLA SHOP

Arranged behind her counter in order of price
were the rows and rows of black umbrellas
I had seen behind her plate glass window
through the driving rain outside. I pointed
toward the cheapest one, a thin fabric
stretched upon a rigid plastic stick,
but she shook her head. — False economy —
she said. — The rain here never stops. You want
one like this, that folds to pocket size,
that fits your glove compartment to take on trips
that everybody takes the first few years:
country drives across the mountain pass
or down the country highway until it widens,
joins the interstate, and, unless you turn
resolutely off at the first exit,
strands you at dawn on unfamiliar ground
like a sleepwalker, blinded by the sun.
You wake, you pull over to the shoulder,
you gaze upon deciduous trees, fleecy
clouds framed in blue, you can't remember
colors or shapes, or even certain names,
like pussywillow. What's that golden thing?
you ask yourself, or the wife beside you
if she hasn't left you yet for Texas.
Or are you already divorced? She asked.
Amazed, I stared into her watery eyes,
but she didn't blink or flinch. She held
the black nylon against her pasty cheek
as if to contrast its color with her skin's
and said: Take this. You're the kind that lasts.

MIGRANT

Finally I understand why geese fly
through clouds of lead pellets
every fall to destinations
they barely remember in their hollow bones:
a few white rocks hissing in the foam;
a palm tree bent away from hurricanes.

If they could talk they'd complain
about the iciness of one home's wind,
about the sadness of the other home's rain,
or explain how each of their feathers
grows a little too thick or too thin
along their poorly adapted wings,

as I, dragging the last box into the van,
explain to the neighbor kid I've paid
all winter to mow the lawn,
how terrible to me his town became
without snow, or restaurants, or sun —
things I despised in the town I came from.

So he asks me why I changed.
I think of flamingos shrugging their wings
in the summer steam, gulls swimming
in the winter foam, and geese
floating through the hunter's gunsight
somewhere in the seven thousand miles between,

considering his question. Given wings,
they've got to fly somewhere perfect
as the sky above the clouds.
That's no place the geese or I have been
except in flight itself,
which gravity makes so difficult

they must, eventually, give their sky up,
circle down through the swarming bullets.
So I tell him his town seemed different
when I saw its dot on my U.S. map:
I admired its distance from the other dots,
its intricate highways in and out.

COMMENTARY ON MIGRANT

I lied in "Migrant" when I said
that geese flew as pointlessly
as I moved in U-Hauls every spring.
They fly in tight formation,
as if the sky were tracked,
from summer corn to winter wheat,
and leave no spaces for the lost.

The bird I watch today
outside my mortgaged study window
makes the backyard tree his home
beneath his business in the sky.
His take-offs and his landings
with twigs lodged in his beak
illustrate the meanness of his wings.

He's building a shaky nest to fill
with children, and he'll teach them
to do the same. He'll wake me
Sunday mornings instead of my alarm,
patrolling borders with his song, flying
no higher than my daughter's kite
if the wind holds out this morning.

Already she's cleared the highest branches.
Will she reel it in, or let it slip
to see if gravity's reversed
on the other side of treetops?
It might fly higher than the geese,
farther, never cross the same sky twice.
In thirty years I own this house.

THE CLIMBER

I'm sitting in my lawn chair tanning,
sipping lemonade and reading
Travel & Leisure's October feature —
Jet Set Beaches Lower Prices —
when neighbor children burst out doors
squealing and diving into leaf piles
raked up just for them to play in.

Imaginary Riviera
laps around my patio,
but snow is falling in their minds.
The last I looked the leaves were green,
but I hear the oldest boy complain
that brown and brittle leaves outnumber
the brilliant red ones still on trees.

I stare hard at my page,
desperately ignoring them.
They're just literary kids
wearing Ode-to-Autumn T-shirts —
the kind who hum Vivaldi's "Seasons"
on their way to private music lessons.
But my summer concentration's gone.

For when I think of my normal childhood,
as crude and genuine and brutal
almost as a Zola novel,
I remember, without nostalgia,
I too anticipated winter.
I was eager for any future,
which I imagined as a ladder

of upward years. I'd get smarter,
richer, handsomer, and farther
from my awful neighborhood
each rung, until, looking down,
I wouldn't see the ground at all.
I wasn't wrong. I've climbed the ladder
of money, class, art, knowledge,

until at forty I'm almost level
with the ten year old next door in culture.
I'm lean and tan, almost, as him.
But while he dives and rolls in leaves,
I grasp the lawn chair's arms like rungs:
the waves out there are really clouds;
my ladder, propped on nothing, sways.

III

METAMORPHOSIS

I watch you feel the dark before you
and test the floor with tips of toes
for shoes and cats and cat toys,

and am reminded of Minefield Practice,
a gradeschool game with firecrackers
I played so badly in the Army

I always stumbled on a trip wire
and had to join the clumsy dead,
who watched by sideline markers

successful players ballet past.
They never fully planted weight,
and trod the air above the grass —

bullies, jellybeans, and louts
all alchemized into dancers.
Imagine, then, the transformation

of a lovely, absentminded woman
concentrating all her grace
so as not to stumble in the dark,

undressed and haloed in the night light.
Such a miracle seen once
stunned me with magnificence,

but a decade's trained me not to blink,
so that my three thousandth glimpse
transfigures me more than did my first.

ROLLER COASTER

The lines are long; the ride's short;
but we'd wait all day for that moment,
hung on the first hill's crest,
when we see the awful downslope.
The endless climb up groaning track
we waste anticipating the drop;
the remainder of the ride we moan;
but in this momentary pause
the droner, old whiner in our heads,
forgets one sentence of his speech

about hunger, thirst, pain, revenge.
His echoes die in our skulls' domes,
and his audience, strapped in,
hears the terrible heart's drum,
feels the blood deluging veins,
smells the oxygen in lungs,
tastes the mouth's weak acid,
and sees the ivory-jointed framework
rock and quiver, way below:
Then our lovely bodies fall.

MY TROPHY

You'd think, instead of ten years,
I won it centuries ago.
The little bronze man on top
is dressed in out-of-fashion togs;
the rivets in his feet are loose
so that he wobbles on his base.
But though the pedestal is tarnished,
my electroplated name and date
and silly praise for my achievement
still legibly announce that miracle:
loss and failure failed me once.
I did best or second best
in a measured competition,
so that ever afterwards
the tiny stadium in my brain
rings with cheers, and always losing,
I always think that I will win.
That feeling's undiminished now
by lead November light that spreads
dully over the fluted handles
and turns the little bronze man green.
My mark is probably surpassed —
someone's loved his wife deeper,
worked harder for less money —
but I'm still drunk, a decade later,
with the thought I thought back then:
even in my studio apartment,
even in my mausoleum,
there will always be a trophy room.

APOLOGY

The war is fought by soldiers in machines
manufactured by their wives: steel skin,
for example, impervious to a caress.
But I am single. I line up with conscripts.
I'm issued sleep confiscated from a civilian
in a safe country. I'm handed a photograph
of his lover to tape inside my locker.
I'm marched to a bed too narrow for her
and me and him together, though he lies
inside me, though she's very slender.
How heavy this green blanket
lies against my neck! How could this rifle!
I'm told the dream which he surrendered,
half in one ear, half in the other,
about Alaska. But it twists inside me.
Which of us is wolf? Which caribou?
Which the tundra? Nobody volunteers his throat,
his appetite, or his cold white isolation
for the sake of peace to anybody else tonight.
We circle on the snow, but the snow drifts over.

I wake beside you thousands of mornings later
when a sergeant shakes my shoulder
to ask if I want a kiss. If it seems too rough,
too desperate for one night's separation
with only sleep between us, excuse me,
there was a war lost and almost a soldier
with it, not in the jungle with the rest,
but solitary, hunted, on the ice.

VALENTINE

Today I rise alone
and tiptoe down the stairs
to release impatient cats
who hate to sleep warm nights.
They're waiting at their door
when I let them out,
their blanket beds unslept in,
their toys flung here and there.
When I raise the blinds
in the living and dining rooms,
I see through muddy panes
cardinals in pairs
on branches and on clotheslines.
When I reach the kitchen
and flick the light switch on,
ants scurry in the sink
for the first time since autumn.
The window thermometer
says fifty-two degrees;
the kitchen calendar
says five weeks till spring.
But my weather radio,
which I flick on to hear
a forecast of fine weather
predicts, instead, a cold front
accompanied by a snowstorm,
and issues livestock warnings
and travelers' advisories.
I curse, and sadly place
my corny heart-shaped box
of chocolates on the tray
beside the toast and coffee,
and trudge back up the stairs.

I find you half awake,
the blanket flung aside,
cats rolling at your feet,
holding out a box
identical to mine.
More snow, I almost tell you,
but manage to shut up.
For inside, winter started
when the ants gave up;
outside, winter ends
when cardinals think it's over.
An avalanche of cats,
a blizzard of warm kisses —
when we trade our candy hearts
we invert the world's climate.

THE SPIDER

I weave my cobweb fingers into the lace.
The pattern's a map of disaster — a fly's
panicked dance, a widow's face reflected
in her mirror; or a ladder for the insane,
who like to climb in circles; or the random
tangle of string on string a seamstress makes,
rummaging the drawer for the shroud needle,
the white thread. Up close, I look like a hanging
suicide in a dead calm, not swaying or turning.
I'm waiting for you to flatten me
against the wall. I'm trying to resemble
a knot in the skein, an error in my work,
a half-eaten wasp whose guts unwind
in every direction, not worth rescue or burial.
If I were you, I'd start to jerk my hands
in rings like a harpist playing for his dinner,
the meat so rare it twitches. Come closer.
I'm your bad dream about what's in corners,
cracks in the surface, up dark alleys.
I like to sting in rhythm with the victim,
who stumbles out my music by mistake
on wires so fragile they bend from breath
and break against the thistles in your broom,
until he moves dream-slow into my mouth.
Now I'm reading the lines in your thumb.
What delicacy! What intricate whorls!

FLORIDA AUBADE

December first in Indiana
sleety rain, driven by wind,
freezes to my bedroom window
so that my view of leafless branches
is distorted by a double glass,
like my diver's view of coral
in the Gulf of Mexico last June,

except that this view's monochrome,
while the wavery bottom of that sea
rainbowed in my flashlight's beam.
The pinkish branches of dead coral,
ornamented with blue crabs
and strung with purple, darting eels,
distracted me from treasure hunting,

because the coins that I was after
had blackened centuries ago.
Dazzled by the yellow sparks
that flashed around the scarlet crayfish —
schools of bright, abundant Jacks
glittering like precious metal —
I blinked and repeated to myself

instructions from the DIVER'S HANDBOOK:
underwater, gold is dark
and silver only shines when scraped
and brass films over as fast as sharks
pick drowned sailers to their bones.
In fact, only sailers shine
here brighter than in native air:

With spongy flesh all stripped away,
with tarnished rings and bracelets slipped
from fingers and from wrists by current
or by the playful cuttlefish,
they take on an ivory sheen
that lasts until the seaweed ropes
re-clothe their bones in dull green suits

after they've shed their cloaks of skin.
But playing my light across the reef
I saw no men, no coins, no wreckage
but the hollowed, cracked shells
snagged on coral spikes: conch
and whelk and butterfly and olive.
I scooped a handful into my sack.

and surfaced with them, my only treasure —
the gaudy bones of brainless sailors
who felt no agony of hope
as storms or enemies smashed their hulls.
The shells were worthless. Now, they sit
in a worthless clear-glass antique dish
on my sill, and are the only colors

I see today in Indiana.
The maple branches against the sky
are gray on darker gray. I rise
and walk naked to my window
and hold the dish up to the light
that leaks through clouds, ice, old glass:
O Florida! O florid death!

THRENODY FOR SUNRISE

Please, when you ask me in this dream
distracting you from the tapping sound of rain
against your opened screen, why we dress
so lightly for your dream's cold wind, listen
carefully to my answer. It will be scrambled,
half drowned by the rattling of your pane.
You'll have to lean completely off your balance
toward my face, grasping my thin lapels.

I think, at the altitude that we'll meet,
my suit of customary black, your blanket,
will be less cold and strange and useless
than the formal greatcoats made of clouds
we wore in dreamless sleeps. They dragged behind,
erasing footprints with their swallow tails.
How often you brushed against me in the dark
looking for sleep's exit! You'd wake, forget

that the clear divisions of day from night
cage you in two adjoining soundproof cells.
If one seems better furnished and better lit,
think how spacious, how possible to hide in,
how few the regulations enforced in sleep.
I've watched you lounging in the vestibule
waiting for the gate to open or to shut
and thought — what if the lock sticks?

Wouldn't you prefer the dream, the wings?
I wish I could have asked before tonight
or that the rain would change to snow, reseal
your window's cracks to block the gray dawn
that's just about to drag across your face.
Please don't press a mirror to your mouth
before I draw the sheet over it —
just hold the light, the heat, the breath.

THRENODY FOR SUNSET

It's five o'clock. Someone's taped my name out
above my timecard's slot. I search the rack,
touching hands that reach around me deftly
punching in or out — dayshift, nightshift,
a card between each steady thumb and finger.
My hand trembles becaues there's nothing in it.
I squeeze the cold iron handle of my lunchbox
to stop the rattle in its empty thermos.

Tonight, there seem to be a hundred Chevys
parked where I always park my Chevy.
I choose the one my key fits. It starts,
coughs, and stops, and will not start again,
its guages stuck on empty, on cold, on zero
in the faint green dashboard lights that flicker,
overload their fuses, and go out.
Didn't I fill my gas tank just this morning?

I walk reluctantly to the locked gate,
whose attendant seems to be asleep.
He doesn't stop me, he doesn't wave me through.
I wait. It's almost dark. Red clouds reflect
against the eastern window of the plant.
Through it, when I squint and stare obliquely,
I see the outline of my black machine
against the blacker shadow of the skyline.

I see a light that might be the first star
or the bedroom lamp from my distant high apartment —
my wife undressing for her bath, singing —
appear inside the dimming clouds' reflection.
I walk toward it, but when I press my face
against the chilly pane, it disappears,
just as she drops her nightgown. I see, instead,
a fading smudge of breath against the glass,

which blocks, for half a second, the constellation
that fills the window of my night replacement.

OUR REWARD

In hell it's always fifty-five degrees
under gray sky. We live in pastel bungalows
next door to whining cocker spaniels,
across from powerful stereos.
Every day is Sunday: the stores closed,
the enormous paper with every bowling score
and the standings of World Team Tennis
reported in the Sports; Dagwood the only comic;
and thirty pages of medical advice
to the dead who want to die twice.

The gray light fades at six o'clock.
Each night we may choose a channel
to watch our re-run *Charlie's Angels*.
Next door, the devils shake their cocktails
in a silver cup. How thin our walls!
I can hear the olive collide with ice
in each chilled glass. I hear sips.
The sound of fingers grazing nylon,
then thighs, under a cotton skirt.
Tonight, they'll laugh past midnight.

Now, at last, it's quiet, and though
we never touch, each undresses in the dark
and lies naked beside a naked lover
on cold sheets. We have no sex,
and though our eyelids never shut,
why should we look at each other?
Nothing ruffles our perfect breasts.
Each of us is heartless, and love
worse torture to us corpses
than death, our substitute for sleep.

VAN GOGH'S POSTHUMOUS CAREER

Through mausoleum bars the grays of sky
at first depressed me, because I thought
to always see blue with one bird, my soul,
balanced, as if on strings, motionless
in the center of my window. Instead
I see clouds only, colored like my walls
but moving. I'm still. All spin
a thousand miles an hour
around a common axis: my sun
would only seem to rise and set if clouds,
which only seem to run faster, farther
than I can, would shift themselves beyond
my six square inch horizon. Tonight,
my three stars won't appear. Years ago
one of them exploded; years from now
I'll see the flash and think
how light crawls over space more slowly
than my confinement, how disaster creeps
compared to my life sentence, to clouds
which blot entire skies out in minutes,
and to my imagination, which years ago
drew clear sky, a bird, and sun
on every wall but the windowed one,
and then erased them all and drew
an imitation of the one I saw.
I call it Sky With Stars. To you,
a blank gray canvas. To me it's clouds
obscuring three points of light, or two,
depending on the night — or if it's dawn,
I see my soul blocking out my sun,
all stars blinded by its enormous wings.

KAFKA BY THE SEA

When I retire, the dead files clerk
will stick my records in the K's: released.
Cashed checks first, then spent vacations
such as this one, whose every martini by the sea
I sign for indelibly in ink, though I will remember
the waitress only, beautiful in this sunset,
who lays it carefully on my cracked plate.
He'll staple each voucher to its invoice,
retrieving the temporary clips that held
my future to its past, my last raise
to my next, for he'll be promoted to my place,
and I to the highest civilian rank,
for which no record's kept.

                    No nameplate will interrupt
the enormous empty surface of my desk.
Waves will break over it, each striving to replace
the last and leave the deepest indentation
in its marble top, and I shall mark down each
that hisses farther than the rest:
to my chin; sometimes to my lips
as if to kiss me for my patience
in waiting out the sunset. I shall file them
by the first letters of their last names —
the waves, the waitress, the whiteness of her skin.
Those are the records that will keep on going
endlessly, in their cabinets of sand.

ELEGY IN A PET CEMETERY

Cut in granite or in sandstone
the names of parakeets and hamsters,
monkeys, goldfish, cats, and chipmunks
depress me, though I came to laugh.

Poll and Nippy and Pretty Boy
no longer beat against their cages;
Sassafras and Cleopatra
don't test upholstery with their claws,

and where are Ginny, Tip, and Spot?
Not barking endlessly all night.
Not chasing mailmen off their porches.
Their headstones say that they are sleeping,

or that they've run to fetch the wind.
None say that they have gone to heaven,
not even dog or woodchuck heaven.
I suppose that lie's forbidden.

Nor are there angels here, or crosses,
for animals are not, like us,
capable of self-transcendence.
Their bodies fit their souls as lace

surrounds the pattern of its holes;
they unravel at their deaths.
Nor are they capable of repentence
for breaking all of the ten commandments.

Thus in hell we can't expect
amid the grit and smoking rocks
the velvet consolation of cats
to smooth our burning hands across,

nor can we who go to heaven
hope to be eased from the endless boredom
of giving perpetual adoration
by dogs who fawn on us in turn.

Neatly laid in rows and columns
like indigent soldiers killed in war,
their markers each are standard-sized,
for they are no more than broken toys —

mangled dolls and teddy bears.
We weep like children for their loss,
but attend real funerals in silence
in the shadows of our monuments.

CONCERTS

1. SCHUBERT'S GREAT SYMPHONY

The audience is so eager to applaud
it listens only for the last note.
I cannot concentrate on music either,
turning pages for the soloist
who dozes during rests. All around,
intent on slivers of the melody,
oboists and kettle drummers play
or poise above their instruments,
inattentive to the violins.
Everyone is staring at the rostrum
where the person paid to blend the sound
wavers torturously above the stage
modulating strings and brass and woodwinds,
hearing variations, not the tune.
Its composer, naturally, is dead,
and while he lived he never could persuade
an orchestra to play his masterpiece —
too new, too strange, and far too difficult.
Now it's played almost every night
to halls as crowded and as deaf as this.

2. BLUEBEARD'S CASTLE

On the planetarium's ceiling
seven doors were slide-projected
onto December's constellations
above the plastic rock escarpments.
Seven giant cardboard keys,
which the baritone clutched limply,
were stolen by the big soprano,
for she was stronger and more talented.
But no one present paid attention
to his shallow voiced refusal
or her resonant insistance
that their marriage have no secrets.

Instead, we listened for the grate
of tape-recorded keys in locks
and watched the slide show overhead
concretize the rooms of treasure
as diamond necklaces on naked breasts,
skeletons to stand for death.
I played the scratchy Bartok record,
our dull but necessary music.

3. OUTDOOR CHRISTMAS CONCERT

The choir is robed in black
to sing medieval carols
no one ever sings,
but the audience consists
of old and homesick tourists.
I'm instructed to announce
during intermission
that it's snowing in Duluth
and ice is snarling Boston.
At this they start to sing
"White Christmas" on their own
without academic training
or orchestra to back them,
for the desert all around
denies that even rain
will fall on us this evening;
therefore the youthful chorus
marches back to stations
to revive the hymnody
of blood and wounds and death.

4. UNHEARD MELODY

When neighbor signals lonely neighbor
on CB radio,
good-by Mozart string quartet
pianissimo.

So I wrap the micro-speakers
in styrofoam
and play the record in my brain
from memory.
But the channels in my ears,
impervious
to local signal's interference,
hear other music —
not the blood tide's echoed roar
in violins
but the repititious drumsong,
heartbeats,
that say *o why, o why, o why*
until they stop,
transcribed into piano by Chopin
as *Requiem*.

5. CODA

(for my stepfather)

Stanley asked if the Military Band
would play a Resurrection song at graveside
to mask the squeaking of the pulley ropes
when we lowered his coffin to the ground.

I told him he'd been dead for many years,
had died in winter time in Baltimore,
as was predicted in recurrent nightmares
that woke him screaming *Jesus, Jesus, no.*

He said that now he didn't dream at all
since everything we awkward dreamers do
so hesitantly — fly without wings, forget our names,
disconnect our bodies from our minds —

he was bored with doing all the time.
When he closed his eyes these days, he said,
they saw exactly what they saw when open.
Dirt? I asked. *The rusted coffin lid?*

Have someone play trombone for me, he said.
Mute cornets. A choir of all-base voices.
And so I croon this morning, *swing low, swing low*
above the ugly moaning of the wind.

EINSTEIN'S BRAIN

> This is the ship of pearl . . .
> — Oliver Wendell Holmes

Instead of spacious chambers furnished
wall to wall in High Victorian
and ceilings hung with chandeliers,
his sectioned neuron passageways,
like this Danish Modern room
where I wait for my optometrist,
disguise great wealth with simpleness.

From blurry newsprint I make out
that the undissected "gross" resembled
average healthy specimens,
and the only inward variation
detectable on dye-soaked slides
is constriction of the tiny veins
such as occurs in all old men

and women. In me, now or soon.
I shift again on hard cushions
and turn the page to smeared pictures
of bits preserved in Mason jars:
Cerebral Cortex, Cerebellum,
Aortic Vessels. Old but normal.
I wonder as I read the labels,

Is my brain ordinary too?
At nine I read "The Chambered Nautilus"
and always, since, imagined brains
created rooms inside their skulls
and moved away when rooms got small.
At twelve I'd add on algebra,
at twenty, calculus, et cetera.

But now the vacant halls behind
seem larger and more sumptuous
than this latest, narrow cell.
Math is gone, and so's religion;
the balcony doors to hope are stuck;
my passions' closet stands ajar,
its secret recess swept and empty.

Of course this space is temporary.
The next apartment of my brain
might have cathedral ceilings domed
with alabaster, stained-glass windows
to rediffuse the pale brilliance
focused by my new spectacles
into spectroscopic light.

*   *   *

*Unlimited Attic or Basement Storage!
The Ultimate in Soundproof!* I blink,
and see I've turned to classifieds:
For Rent, Studios, Unfurnished.
I used to always read Help Wanted
to see if work that I could do
was advertised. It never was.

So now I look through Real Estate
for a quiet, safe apartment
to move to if my mortgage lapses
on my too-expensive house.
I'd like a single room, high up,
with one window and one door,
to let in air, to bar at night,

with bone-white walls and no pictures
to interrupt the classic blankness.
I'd be the perfect tenant — silent,
friendless, no children, no pets,
who'd read the morning paper all day,
keeping up with every story
of spectacular public failure.

At night I'd only dream a life
full of sex and violence
but absolutely noiseless, I promise.
Nobody'd hear its background music,
although it deafens me at times
with its swelling violins
and its syncopated horns.

Sounds must dampen down to nothing
within the windings of my ears
because their point of origin's
inside my involuted brain.
The constant buzz of bad ideas
is tightly stoppered by my eardrums:
just now I thought I wope up screaming

when this newspaper slipped my grasp
and crashed so loudly to the floor,
but the appointment clerk still files her nails,
and the old and nearly blind bus driver
still desperately squints at the eye chart.
I guess he fears a forced retirement —
all that time to just think.

*　　*　　*

DOCS SAY GENIUS' BRAIN WAS NORMAL
I read as I refold the paper.
But his webbed and fluted filament,
shell-shaped, incurving,
was once an extraordinary skull's
frail tenant; what *lies revealed*,
its irised ceiling rent, is wreckage

from the awful inward voyage
of his mollusk-like intelligence
within the shell curved small and low
to prevent its shrunken cargo
from shifting in that final storm
he had to sail into, as I will,
with imperfect instruments.

My hearing dulls; my eyes get worse;
I often find myself, like now,
vacantly waiting for repairs.
I'm not comforted by comparisons:
if my skull's an ocean liner,
my brain's an ailing mariner
no longer interested in seas;

if my skull's a tenement,
my brain's its unambitious builder
satisfied with maintenance.
But architect or shipwright,
here's the shell my brain's devised:
deposited in surf-torn sand,
abandoned by its occupant.

Your eyes, I know, are drawn toward
that glittering row of new hotels,
those yachts bobbing at their anchors,
and the beautiful, nearly naked swimmers
churning through the smooth water,
but please don't crush my Nautilus
absentmindedly in your palm.

The work's old fashioned, over-wrought.
The workman, caught in curving space,
and, even with new glasses, blind,
crept along its convolutions
with just himself for trowel and mortar.
But ordinary as it looks,
inside it once was universe.

ACKNOWLEDGMENTS

Some of the poems which appear here have been published in the following magazines and are reprinted with permission:

AMERICAN POETRY REVIEW: "Abstinence," "Apology," "Concerts," "Einstein's Brain," "The Spider," "Threnody for Sunrise," "Threnody for Sunset," "Widower."

CHOOMIA: "Migrant," "The Airport of the Country of the Blind," "Van Gogh's Posthumous Career."

CRAZYHORSE: "The Interrupted Nap," "The Middle Class," "The Umbrella Shop."

GEORGIA REVIEW: "Fredericksburg."

THE LOUISVILLE REVIEW: "The Climber," "Guilt."

PLOUGHSHARES: "Genre Painting," "Night School."

POETRY: "Elegy in a Pet Cemetery."

POETRY EAST: "Exile."

POETRY NOW: "My Trophy."

SEATTLE REVIEW: "The Relief Map."

SONORA REVIEW: "What Cheer, Iowa."

TAR RIVER POETRY: "Our Reward."

TELESCOPE: "At the Franklin Planetarium."

TENDRIL: "The Wanderer."

VIRGINIA QUARTERLY REVIEW: "Venice."

31100039